Dirty Jokes
Every Man
Should Know

Copyright © 2009 by Quirk Productions, Inc.

Library of Congress Cataloging in Publication Number:
2009924496

ISBN: 978-1-59474-427-3

Printed in China

Typeset in Goudy

Designed by Doogie Horner
Production management by John J. McGurk

20 19 18 17 16 15 14 13 12 11

Quirk Books
215 Church Street
Philadelphia, PA 19106
quirkbooks.com

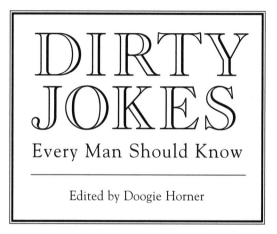

DIRTY JOKES

Every Man Should Know

Edited by Doogie Horner

QUIRK BOOKS

PHILADELPHIA

Table of Contents

Introduction

Hello, dear reader, and welcome to *Dirty Jokes Every Man Should Know*. Not to suck your dick or anything, but I'd like to begin by complimenting you on your good taste and comedic sophistication. You're very brave. A lot of people wouldn't have had the guts to pick up this book. They'd be worried that someone might see them—a coworker, pastor, or old flame—and discover that they're a pervert. But you're not afraid to have everyone at the office know that you enjoy a good queef joke, and I admire you for that. Personally, I'm writing this book under a pseudonym.

Let's not ignore the proverbial elephant with the erect cock in the room—dirty jokes are the black sheep of the joke family. They're the alcoholic, bachelor uncle who is never invited to the family reunion, never mentioned in the annual Christmas letter, and always sets off fireworks in the garage on Christmas morning. But just like our drunk uncle, we all have a secret sweet spot for the dirty joke. Remember that time he took us fishing with dynamite? And taught us how to shoot a gun? He reeked heavily of whiskey, and it was weird when he peed in the Coke bottle while we held the steering wheel, but it was still much more fun than sitting around with the rest of the family playing Scattergories.

The spectrum of dirty jokes is wider than most people realize. If you think all dirty jokes are about fucking sheep, think again! Dirty jokes can be about any subject that's generally considered taboo: sex, profanity, vice, bestiality, religion, bodily functions, substance abuse, nudity, violence, or mocking the elderly, sick, or handicapped. The best dirty jokes, of course, encompass all these subjects.

Just as your besotted uncle still thinks it is 1968 and he's in Cambodia, dirty jokes inhabit their own unique reality. The world of dirty jokes is a gritty jungle where shadows have teeth and anyone, at any moment, could be raped by an escaped gorilla. The malicious hand of fate strikes quickly in these jokes. One moment you're walking down the street, looking in the window of an antique shop at a vase your wife might like, and the next moment a gorilla's balls are deep in your rectum.

Think I'm exaggerating? Here's a typical day in the life of a dirty joke character:

8:00 A.M.: Woke to find my penis had been replaced by an elephant's trunk.

8:01 A.M.: Screamed.

9:00 A.M.: Went to doctor, who laughed and tossed me a bag a peanuts. Trunk promptly shoved peanuts up my ass.

10:00 A.M.: Returned home to find wife fucking a Shetland pony.

12 noon: Went to my pastor for spiritual guidance—discovered he's balling my wife as well.

1:00 P.M.: Shit peanut shells for four hours.

5:00 P.M.: Went to bar. Sat between an alligator and a hamburger who wouldn't shut up.

7:00 P.M.: Found a magic lantern with genie
        inside.

7:05 P.M.: Transported to deserted island with a
        Pole and an Italian.

10:00 P.M.: Eaten by giant clam.

There's no safe place in these jokes. They're Lovecraftian tales of horror crossed with postmodern, slice-of-life short stories: A man wakes up, goes to take a shower, and menstrual blood pours out of the faucet. End of story. Given the bizarre circumstances in these jokes, the punch line is almost incidental.

This brings us to another crucial difference between dirty and clean jokes: most dirty jokes don't end well. When a story begins, "So this guy is blowing a duck . . ." it's hard to imagine a happy ending.*

---

*Okay, I'll try: Since the guy blowing the duck has a pure heart, the Red Witch's curse is finally lifted, and the duck transforms back into a handsome prince. The two become best friends, return to the prince's kingdom to reclaim his father's throne from the Dark Lord Obelon and restore peace to his people. They also open a lucrative duck farm.

This pinch of salt gives dirty jokes an extra kick because it throws the humor into sharper contrast. If you lick an ice cream cone, it will taste pretty good. But if you lick a piece of shit, and then lick the ice cream cone, the ice cream will taste fabulous, and you can easily win five bucks on the dare. The sweet-and-sour mixture of dirty jokes operates on this same principle, known in academic circles as the "poopy," or "shit-lick," principle.

The extra helping of tragedy in dirty jokes also elevates them above their fundamental dirtiness by eliciting pathos. After we're done laughing at the unfortunate woman with the voodoo dick stuck in her pussy (see page 50), we feel sympathy for her—and then we start laughing again and tell the joke to our cellmate.

I have, by now, irrefutably proven that dirty jokes are a far more complex, rich mode of artistic expression than you previously understood. But so is ballet, and I know you don't give a shit about that. Why is it important that you know the dirty jokes in this book?

First of all, ballet is for girls. I'm surprised you even mentioned it—makes me wonder if you're queer. Secondly, although the jokes in this book are undoubtedly dirty, it's important to understand that dirt isn't always a bad thing. Did you know that hippos roll in dirt to keep themselves cool and to protect their skin from sunburn? In the same way, rolling in these dirty jokes—laughing at the characters' sad foibles and gasping at their outlandish predicaments—may help shield you from life's little daily misfortunes. Like taking a greedy lick of a fresh, steaming shit casserole, reading these jokes really puts things in perspective: No matter how bad your day has been, at least you're not trapped in a barrel, giving blow jobs to lumberjacks.*

---

*And even if you are, this book can still help you, by blocking the hole everyone's sticking their dicks through. Or maybe you should just go get your G.E.D., cocksucker.

The bashful bride and groom were delighted to be finally alone in their honeymoon suite. Blushing, the bride asked her new husband, "Johnny, now that we're married, could you tell me what a penis is?"

Pleased to discover his wife was a virgin, he took out his penis and showed it to her.

"Oh," she said, "it's just like a dick, only smaller."

While walking across the moors one lonely night, two sheep herders found an extremely sexy ewe. One of the herders climbed on and started humping when the sheep stuck its tongue out.

"Damn!" the other herder said, "Your dick's coming out the other end!"

"Then stick on another sheep!"

An old cowboy is sitting at the bar when a beautiful young woman sits down next to him and orders a drink.

"You're a mighty pretty gal," the cowboy says. "How'd you like to go dancin' with a real cowboy?"

"Are you really a cowboy?" the woman asks.

"Shucks, I'd say so. Been tending cows my whole life. First thing when I wake up in the morning, I herd cows. All day long I herd cows. In the evening I herd cows. Heck, when I sleep at night, I even dream about herdin' cows!" He winks at her. "Now, how'd you like to get to know a real cowboy?"

"I'm not interested," the woman says. "I'm a lesbian."

The old cowboy is shocked. "A lesbian? Are you sure?"

"I'm pretty sure. First thing when I wake up in the morning, I think about licking pussy. All day long I think about licking pussy. In the evening I think about licking pussy. When I sleep at night, I even dream about licking pussy."

With that she drains her drink, gets up, and leaves the bar.

A guy sits down in her empty seat and notices the cowboy staring morosely into his drink. "Hey," he says, "are you a real cowboy?"

"Well, I used to think so," the cowboy says. "But apparently I'm a lesbian!"

An old couple met for a romp

in the broom closet at the retirement home.
They undressed and were about to fuck when
the woman realized she should warn the man
of her heart condition.

"I should tell you," she said, "I have acute
angina."

The man replied, "That's good, because
you have the ugliest breasts I've ever seen!"

This guy goes to a whorehouse.

The madam takes him upstairs and escorts him into a room with a hooker, who proceeds to tell him the prices. "For five dollars we can do it on the floor," she says. "It's ten dollars to do it on the couch, and twenty if you want to do it on the bed."

The guy hands her a twenty.

"Good choice," she says, and hops on the bed.

"No, no," the guy says, "I want four on the floor."

An old gentleman marries a lady

who is much younger than he is. They love each other very much, but their sex life is bad. No matter how hard the husband tries, his wife never reaches orgasm. They decide to go to a marriage counselor to ask for advice.

The counselor says, "Hire a strong young man. While the two of you are making love, have the young man give your wife a foot massage. That will help her relax and should bring on an orgasm."

They go home and follow the counselor's advice. They hire a handsome young man and he massages the wife's feet while they make love. However, it doesn't help, and she is still unable to climax.

They return to the counselor. "Okay," the counselor says to the husband, "let's reverse it. Have the young man make love to your wife while you massage her feet." So they go home and follow the counselor's advice.

The young man gets into bed with the

wife while the husband massages her feet. The young man is very enthusiastic; he makes love to the wife with skill and grace. His firm muscles knead her supple flesh. She bites his shoulder and draws blood. They devour each other like hungry animals, and after a half hour of intense pumping and moaning, the wife has an ecstatic, screaming orgasm that starts the neighbor's dog barking and sets off every car alarm on the block.

The husband smiles, looks at the young man, and says triumphantly, "See, asshole? *That's* how you give a foot massage!"

Three guys go to a ski lodge. There aren't enough rooms, so they have to share a bed for the night. In the morning, the guy on the right wakes up and says, "Last night I had the wildest, most vivid dream that I was getting a hand job!"

The guy on the left wakes up and says, "That's incredible. I had the exact same dream!"

The guy in the middle wakes up last and says, "Boy, I'm really excited to hit the slopes. Last night I had the most realistic dream that I was skiing!"

The doctor wanted to write a prescription, so he reached in his pocket and pulled out a thermometer. "Shit," he said, "some asshole has my pen."

When Are These Jokes Appropriate?

Now that you have this slim, stylish volume of dirty jokes, I know you will be eager to show it off. After all, it fits comfortably in your back pocket or hollow wooden leg, and you're sure that the diarrhea hair gel joke will go over big at brunch.

Stop. Right. There.

You can't tell diarrhea jokes at brunch. Well, you can, but everyone will lose their appetite and leave their crêpes unfinished, and you will never be invited to brunch again. Once your shawl-of-the-month knitting club catches wind of the scandal, they may even give you the cold shoulder. How well a dirty joke is received has as much to do with where you tell it as how you tell it. The same ribald jape that bombed at brunch will elicit gales of laughter when told at a fraternity brother's wake.

Knowing a dirty joke (or a hundred, you lucky

dog) is like knowing how to give the Heimlich maneuver or a rim job: It's an impressive skill, but you have to wait for the right moment to administer it, otherwise you look like a knucklehead. In the same way that sex is best when shared during the bond of marriage or with a masked stranger on a vibrating bed dusted with cocaine, dirty jokes are best when shared with the right people, at the right time, in the right situation.

Because everyone loves parables (any apostles in the crowd?), let me put it another way: Dirty jokes are like orchids; they require a unique set of circumstances to bloom. Dirty jokes are not like Chia Pets, which can flourish on a sunny windowsill or in a dark closet. For a dirty joke to elicit honest, cathartic laughter, it must be told in exactly the right circumstances. And just like an orchid, when told properly, a dirty joke will eerily resemble the female genitalia.

How well you know your audience can supersede the appropriateness of the location. For instance, you can tell a good friend a dirty joke during his child's christening, but you should only tell an absolute stranger a dirty joke in a more casual setting, such as a bar or hootenanny.

Use this state-of-the-art gauge to estimate whether or not you're in the right place to engage in raunchy raillery.

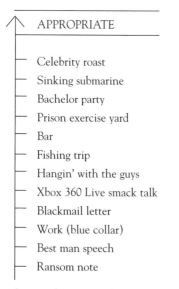

APPROPRIATE

- Celebrity roast
- Sinking submarine
- Bachelor party
- Prison exercise yard
- Bar
- Fishing trip
- Hangin' with the guys
- Xbox 360 Live smack talk
- Blackmail letter
- Work (blue collar)
- Best man speech
- Ransom note

(continued on next page)

— Lunch
— Work (white collar)
— Brunch
— Dinner with parents
— Job interview
— Church/synagogue/mosque/Satanic shrine
— Bhat Mitzvah
— Heaven
— Congressional hearing
— Impeachment trial

∨ INAPPROPRIATE

A gorgeous woman walks up to the bar in a quiet rural pub. She gestures alluringly to the barman, who comes over immediately. When he arrives, she seductively beckons him closer. He leans his face close to hers, and she begins to gently caress his full, bushy beard.

"Are you the manager?" she asks, softly stroking his face with both hands.

"Actually, no," he replies.

"I need to tell him something," she says, pouting, running her hands up through his beard and into his hair. "Can you get him for me?"

"I'm afraid I can't," breathes the barman. He's clearly aroused. "Is there anything I can do for you?"

"Yes there is. I need you to give him a message," she continues huskily, popping a couple of fingers into his mouth and allowing him to suck them gently. "Tell him there's no toilet paper in the ladies room."

Two couples got together every Saturday night for years, but their visits were starting to get boring. One night, after several drinks, they decided to spice things up by swapping partners.

The next morning, Mike woke up, rolled over and asked, "Did you enjoy that?"

"I had a terrific time," his new partner replied. "Let's go see how the girls did."

After a particularly wild company Christmas party, the vice president woke up with a terrible hangover. He turned over and groaned to his wife, "What in the hell happened last night?"

"As usual, you made a fool of yourself in front of the chairman of the board."

"Piss on him," the man answered.

"You did," she said. "And he fired you."

"Fuck him," the man replied.

"I did. You go back to work on Monday."

A little boy walked into the bathroom just as his mother was stepping out of the shower. He stared in wonder at the black triangle of fur between her legs and asked, "Mommy, what's that?"

The mother stammered for a moment, then said, "Why, honey, that's my black sponge."

The answer satisfied the little boy, and the mother hoped he wouldn't mention it again. Later that day though, when the mother was in the kitchen, the boy came up to her and asked, "Mommy, I spilled some milk. Can I borrow your black sponge?"

The mother thought fast and said, "Sorry dear, I've lost it."

The boy walked away. A couple minutes later he dashed back into the kitchen and said, "Mommy, Mommy, I've found your black sponge! Mrs. Johnson next door is cleaning Daddy's face with it!"

A young priest was startled to hear the confession of a very young girl who said that her sin was that she loved to suck cocks. Unsure of the proper penance for such an unusual confession, the young priest excused himself and went back into the vestry to tell the monsignor what he'd heard.

"That must be Carolyn Jones," the monsignor said.

"So you've heard her confession, too," the young priest said. "What did you give her?"

"Ten dollars," the monsignor replied. "Though you can probably get away with five."

God decided he needed a vacation.
One of his angels suggested Mercury. "No
thanks," God said. "I went there 20,000 years
ago and got sunburned."

Another angel suggested Pluto. "Forget it,"
God replied. "I went there 10,000 years ago and
froze my ass off."

A third angel suggested Earth. "That's the
worst," God answered angrily. "I was there
2,000 years ago, and they're still accusing me
of knocking up some Jewish chick."

A ninety-five-year-old man went to the doctor and said, "Doctor, my twenty-one-year-old wife is pregnant."

"Let me tell you a story," the doctor said. "A man went hunting. But instead of a gun, he accidentally picked up an umbrella. When a bear burst out of the woods and charged him, he picked up his umbrella, shot the bear, and killed it."

The man said, "Well, that's impossible. I think someone else must have shot that bear."

The doctor said, "Exactly!"

Dirty Willie Nelson Jokes

Dirty jokes are only one small part of the ever-expanding joke universe: puns, limericks, impersonations, observational humor, political humor, knock-knock jokes, and riddles are all galaxies in a hilarious sky that stretches to infinity. Within the dirty joke solar system, there are planets and satellites: dirty religious jokes, dirty handicapped jokes, dirty sex jokes, and so on. (Scientists are still vigorously debating whether shit-eating jokes are a planet or satellite.)

During my exhaustive research for this book, I probed deep into the world of dirty jokes and discovered ever smaller, more specialized dirty joke subsets. Like the strange, luminous fish that live on the ocean's floor, far below the depths most creatures can survive, the dirty jokes found at the far end of the spectrum often develop in surprising and—some would say—unnatural ways.

Nowhere is this perversion more shocking than with the rarest of all dirty joke subcategories: dirty Willie Nelson jokes. And no comic knows more dirty Willie Nelson jokes than Chip Chantry. Chip has worked solely in off-color Willie Nelson jokes for the past 25 years and, in that time, has written or collected the six jokes that follow. Which—as Chip is quick to point out—is six more dirty Willie Nelson jokes than anyone else has bothered to collect.

What's the worst thing Willie Nelson can say while giving you a hand job?

"By the way . . . I'm not really Willie Nelson."

What do you get when you fuck Willie Nelson?

Farm AIDS.

Who did Willie Nelson give herpes to?

All the girls he loved before.

When does Willie Nelson get on the road again?

When he's done Wailin' Jennings.

A woman goes into a tattoo parlor and tells the tattoo artist she wants a portrait of Brad Pitt on the inside of her left thigh and a portrait of Johnny Depp on the inside of her right thigh.

She spreads her legs and the artist tattoos the two portraits on her thighs. When he's done, he stands back and admires his work. "Pretty good, huh?" he says.

The woman looks down and says, "That doesn't look anything like Brad or Johnny!"

The tattoo artist disagrees and suggests they get a second opinion. So he steps outside, grabs a guy off the street, and pulls him into the tattoo parlor.

The woman spreads her legs, and the tattoo artist asks the man, "All right, who does that look like to you?"

The man stares at the woman's loins for a long time, and finally he says, "Well, I don't know who the guys on the left and right are, but that fella' in the middle has got to be Willie Nelson."

Willie Nelson was playing Trigger, his famous guitar that has a large hole in it, for a reporter. The reporter asked him if it was true that he would retire when he made the hole so big he could not play it anymore. "Absolutely," Willie replied.

"Just because you make a huge hole in it means retirement?"

Willie nodded. "Just ask my first three wives."

A man who smoked a dozen cigars a day tried everything to quit, but without success. He finally heard about a doctor who promised a foolproof method.

"You're going to think this is crazy," the doctor said. "But every night before you go to bed, stick a cigar all the way into your rectum. The next morning, pull it out, put it back in the wrapper, and place it with the rest of your stogies. You won't be able to tell which one you stuck up your butt; therefore, you won't smoke any of them."

The man was skeptical, but he gave it a shot. A month later, he went back to the doctor and reported that the treatment had worked, and he'd quit smoking cigars.

"Great," the doctor said. "I'm happy to hear that."

"Yeah, but now I've got another problem."

"What's that?" the doctor asked.

The man replied, "Now I can't fall asleep without sticking a cigar up my ass."

A man went to the doctor for a physical. Halfway through the examination the doctor discovered that the man had dark brown balls.

"I know," the man said. "Don't worry about it."

"I've never seen this before," the doctor said, "I'm going to have to examine further."

"No. Move on with the examination," the man said, visibly uncomfortable.

"But this could be a serious medical problem!" the doctor insisted.

The man got so angry he got up and left.

When he arrived home he was still mad. He shouted to his wife, "This place is a mess. The kitchen is full of dirty dishes, the bedroom's full of dirty clothes, and the kids are filthy."

She yelled back, "You could help me sometimes. I'm so busy I don't have time to wipe my ass."

"That's another thing I want to talk to you about," the man said.

A man goes into the confession booth and tells the priest, "Father, I'm seventy years old and last night I made love to three twenty-one-year-old girls—at the same time."

"When did you last go to confession?" the priest asked.

The man says, "I've never been to confession, Father. I'm Jewish."

"Then why are you telling me?"

The man says, "Are you kidding? I'm telling everybody!"

A female patient has been in a coma for five years. One of the nurses is giving her a sponge bath when she notices a spike in the patient's vital signs. She touches the patient's gentials with the sponge, and the vital signs spike again.

The next day, when the patient's husband visits, the nurse tells him, "I know it sounds crazy, but maybe a little oral sex will bring her out of the coma."

The husband is skeptical, but the staff promises to close the curtains for privacy, and they point out that they don't have much to lose. After a lot of counseling, the husband agrees to give it a shot, and he goes into his wife's room.

After a few minutes the woman's monitor flatlines. She's dead. The doctors and nurses run into the room and find the husband standing there, zipping up his pants.

He says, "I think she choked."

There was an awful mistake at the hospital. A man who was scheduled for a vasectomy was given a sex-change operation instead. The doctors gathered around his recovery bed to break the bad news.

"Ohhhh no!" the patient screamed, "Dear God no! I'll never be able to experience an erection again!"

"Of course you'll still be able to experience an erection," one surgeon said soothingly. "It will just have to be someone else's."

A woman was prescribed male hormones for a rare heart condition. After a few weeks, she became concerned about some of the side effects she was experiencing.

"Doctor," she said, "the hormones have really helped my heart, but I'm afraid that you're giving me too much. I've started growing hair in places I've never grown it before."

The doctor reassured her that a little hair growth was expected due to the increased testosterone in her system. "Where exactly has this hair appeared?"

"On my balls."

A millionaire and his wife lead a lavish lifestyle—until, one day, the guy lost everything in a shady investment deal. That night he went home and explained their diminished financial status to his wife.

"Since we need to start saving, you better learn to cook so that we can let go of our personal chef."

"That's fine," she said. "If you can learn how to fuck, we can fire the gardener, too."

A woman was masturbating a little too vigorously when her vibrator got stuck inside her vagina. No matter how hard she tried, she couldn't get it out. Weeks went by and it still wouldn't budge, so she finally went to the gynecologist.

At the end of the examination, the gynecologist said, "I'm sorry to say that removing this vibrator is going to require a difficult and extensive operation."

"I'm not sure I can afford all that," the woman sighed. "Why don't you just replace the batteries?"

Young Tommy was getting old enough to be curious about the birds and the bees, so when he and his father encountered two dogs humping in an empty lot, his dad explained that they were making puppies.

A week later Tommy stumbled into his parents' room in the middle of the night and caught them having sex. "What are you and Mommy doing?" he asked.

"Well, Billy," the embarrassed father explained, "Mommy and I are making babies."

"Roll her over, Dad!" screamed the little boy, hopping up and down. "I'd rather have puppies!"

A flea had oiled up his little flea arms and legs, spread out his blanket, and he was proceeding to soak up the Miami sun when he saw his old friend Oscar stumbling up the beach.

"Oscar, what happened to you?" asked the flea. Oscar looked terrible; he was wrapped in a blanket—his nose running, eyes red, teeth chattering.

"I got a ride down here in some guy's mustache and he came by motorcycle. I nearly froze my nuts off," wheezed Oscar.

"Let me give you a tip, old pal," said the first flea, spreading some more suntan oil on his shoulders. "You go to the stewardess lounge at the airport, see, and you get up on the toilet seat. When an Air Florida stewardess comes in to take a leak, you hop onto her bush for a nice warm ride. Got it?"

A month or so later, the same flea is stretched out on the beach when he sees Oscar looking more chilled and miserable than before.

"I did everything you told me," said Oscar. "I made it to the stewardess lounge and waited until a really cute one sat down. I hopped onto her, made a perfect landing, and got so warm and cozy that I dozed right off."

"So what happened?" asked the first flea.

"Well, next thing I know, I'm on this guy's mustache again!"

A businessman is about to leave on a long business trip, but he's concerned his wife will cheat on him while he's gone. So he goes to a sex shop to find a toy that will keep her satisfied. He browses the vibrators, the dildos, and the stimulating creams but doesn't see anything that looks like it will satisfy her ravenous sexual appetite. So he consults the old man behind the counter.

"Well," the old man says, "I can only think of one other thing. I don't usually recommend this, but if you're desperate . . ." The old man reaches under the counter and pulls out an old wooden box, carved with arcane runes. He opens it, and inside, on a velvet cushion, lies an ordinary-looking dildo.

"Watch this," says the proprietor. He points to the front door and says, "Voodoo dick, the door." The voodoo dick levitates out of its box, flies over to the door, and starts fucking the shit out of the keyhole. It pounds so hard that the entire frame shakes, and the door starts to split in two.

"Voodoo dick, the box!" the old man commands.

The voodoo dick stops, floats back to its box, and lies quiet once more.

The businessman is ecstatic. "I'll take it!"

When he gets home, he shows the voodoo dick to his wife and tells her, "If you get lonely, all you have to do is say, "Voodoo dick, my pussy." Then he gives her a kiss on the labia and leaves for his business trip.

The wife tries to behave herself, but after a few weeks she grows unbearably horny, so she gives the voodoo dick a try. Feeling a little foolish, she says, "Voodoo dick, my pussy."

The voodoo dick flies out of its box and dives into her pussy. It pounds away with a passion and skill she has never experienced before. She's lifted to unknown heights of ecstasy. After the twelfth orgasm, she decides she's had enough, so she tries to pull the voodoo dick out.

But the voodoo dick won't come out.

The woman tries everything, but the voodoo dick won't stop fucking. Her husband never told her how to stop it! Barely able to stand with the dick still pounding away, she throws on a dress, hops in the car, and heads for the emergency room.

On the way there, a fresh wave of orgasms rocks her body, and her car almost swerves off the road. When she looks in her rearview mirror, she's horrified to see a police car pulling her over.

The policeman strolls up to her window, and observing her disheveled state, asks if she's been drinking.

"No officer," she says, twitching and moaning, "There's a voodoo dick stuck in my pussy, and it won't stop fucking!"

"Sure, lady," says the officer. "Voodoo dick, my ass!"

Three men were sitting sulkily at a bar. The first said, "I hate this dive. I know a place on Broad Street where I can get every third drink free."

"That's nothing," said the second. "I know a joint over on the east side where every other drink is free."

"Oh yeah?" said the third guy, "well I know a place on the north side where every drink is free, and at the end of the night you can get laid in the parking lot!"

"Seriously?" asked his friends. "That sounds great—where'd you hear about it?"

"From my wife," he said proudly.

A famous weight loss doctor prescribes a crash diet to an 800-pound man. The diet works, and a year later the obese man is down to 180 pounds and fit as a fiddle. The only problem is that now his body is draped with droopy folds of flesh where the fat used to be.

The doctor listens to his predicament and tells him not to worry. "We can correct the problem with a simple surgery," the doctor assures him. "Just come over to the clinic."

"But doctor," says the man, "How am I going to get to the clinic? I'm too embarrassed to be seen in public like this."

"Don't worry about it," says the doctor. "Just pull up the folds of fat as high as they'll go. Pile the flesh on top of your head, and put on a hat."

The guy follows the instructions and reaches the clinic without anybody noticing anything out of the ordinary. But as he stands in front of the admitting nurse's desk, dying of self-consciousness, he can feel her eyeing him shrewdly.

"The doctor will be right with you," says the nurse. "Say, what's that hole in the middle of your forehead?"

"My belly button," blurts out the guy. "How do you like my tie?"

Lonely Lumberjack Jokes

A large percentage of dirty jokes involve men and women (usually men) fucking things they shouldn't: hamsters, dogs, horses, pickle slicers, children, corpses, belly buttons, and dolphin blowholes. Most of these jokes were written by the government during WWII (what a great war), and were intended as short parables to discourage enlisted men from contracting venereal disease. After the war, the words "French whores" or "Nazi whores" were simply swapped out of the jokes, and that's how we've come to know the jokes today.

The men in these jokes usually have their back to the wall—they are lonely men driven to desperate extremes. Oh sure, there's the occasional enthusiastic pig fucker, but, for the most part, the characters in these jokes are simple men not unlike you or me, although a lot more like you. You don't want to have sex with a horseshoe crab, but when you're trapped on a desert island and the hermit crabs are too small to fuck, what other choice do you have?

Personally, my favorite subgroup within this genre is the lonely lumberjack jokes. I've never met a lumberjack, but I imagine them as honest, hardworking men. Lumberjacks are like unicorns—even though I'm not sure if they exist, I'm still well versed in their romantic lore: plaid shirts, thick beards, crisp mountain air, and golden, glowing horns. Actually, now that I think of it, if someone wrote a joke about a lumberjack fucking a unicorn, it might be the greatest dirty joke of all time. Please mail your dirty unicorn/lumberjack jokes to:

Doogie Horner
c/o Quirk Books
215 Church St.
Philadelphia, PA 19106

If chosen, your dirty joke may be featured in our next humor anthology: *Lumberjacks Fucking Mystical Beast Jokes Every Man Should Know.*

A new lumberjack had just finished his first month in the lonely woods of Alaska, where there were no women for miles. He was growing incredibly horny, and he asked the foreman what the men did to relieve the pressure.

"Try the hole in the barrel outside the shower," suggested the foreman. "The men swear by it."

The lumberjack was uncertain but desperate, so he tried the barrel—and had the best experience of his life. Afterward he told the foreman, "That barrel is fantastic! I'm going to use it every day!"

"Every day but Monday," the foreman said.

"Why not Monday?"

"Because that's your day in the barrel."

This guy moves to a remote cabin deep in the Alaskan wilderness. He doesn't see another living soul for an entire month until one day there's a knock on his door. Outside he finds a huge, grizzled man, smiling broadly.

"Welcome to the neighborhood!" he says,

sticking out his hand. "My name's Tom. I live on the other side of the mountain. I'm having a party at my cabin tonight, and I wanted to invite you."

"Thanks, I'd love to come."

"I just have to warn you," Tom says. "My parties can get a little wild."

"That's okay."

"Well, sometimes people get drunk, and sometimes a fight breaks out," Tom says sheepishly.

"That's all right too. I can handle myself."

"Just one other thing. Sometimes, at my parties, people get drunk, and maybe start a fight, and then sometimes everybody starts fucking."

"Well, I'm an adult, I don't have problem with that. How many people are going to be there?"

Tom smiles. "Just you and me."

A lumberjack joins a logging crew that's working deep in the wilds of Alaska, miles away from any other towns. When he arrives, he discovers that the only civilization is one muddy street with a grocery store, a general store, and a bar at the end.

He walks into the bar and has a few drinks. He notices there are no women in the bar, only men. "Hey," he asks the bartender, "what do the men do around here for company?"

The bartender looks at the clock and says, "You'll find out at midnight."

The lumberjack is intrigued, so he sticks around.

At the stroke of midnight, everyone in the bar stands up and walks outside. The lumberjack follows them outside. There's a moonlit field filled with moose, and all the guys from the bar are fucking the moose.

The lumberjack is disgusted. He runs back to his cabin and throws up. He wonders how anyone could be horny enough to fuck a moose.

Nine months later, he understands. He hasn't seen a single woman the whole time. He's so horny, he thinks that maybe he could fuck a moose.

He arrives at the bar early and starts drinking heavily. He wants to be completely smashed before midnight. He keeps his eye on the clock, downing shot after shot of whiskey and watching the hands creep implacably towards midnight.

As soon as the clock strikes midnight, he jumps off his stool and runs outside faster than anyone else in the bar. He runs up to the first moose he sees and starts fucking the shit out of it.

He's fucking the moose so vigorously that it takes a few moments before he looks around and realizes none of the other moose are being fucked. He looks behind him and sees all the other lumberjacks from the bar, staring at him in slack-jawed disgust.

"What?" he says. "What's the matter?"

One of the lumberjacks steps forward. "Dude . . . that is the ugliest moose I've ever seen."

A naive young priest moves from the country to a parish in a bad neighborhood of the Bronx. Walking through the neighborhood, he's baffled by the hookers who are constantly approaching him to whisper, "Twenty bucks for a blow job, sweetie."

He has no clue what they're talking about, so he finally approaches one of the nuns.

"Excuse me, Sister," ask the young priest, "but could you please tell me what a blow job is?"

"Twenty bucks," she replies, "same as anywhere else."

The Israelites waited anxiously at the foot of the mountain. They knew Moses had had a tough day negotiating with God over the Commandments.

Finally, an exhausted Moses trudged down the mountain. "I've got some good news and some bad news, folks," he said. "The good news is that I got Him down to ten. The bad news is that adultery is still one of them."

A guy is standing at a urinal when he notices that he's being watched by a midget. The guy starts to get uncomfortable when the midget drags a small stepladder up next to him, climbs it, and proceeds to admire his privates at close range. "Wow," says the midget, "those are the nicest balls I have ever seen!"

Surprised—and flattered—the man thanks the midget.

"Listen, I know this is a strange request," says the midget, "but would you mind if I touched them?"

The man is distinctly uncomfortable, but not wanting to offend the midget, he obliges.

The midget reaches out and gets a tight grip on the man's balls. He turns to the man and dangles one foot over the edge of the ladder, "Okay, hand over your wallet or I jump!"

A man at a nudist camp got a letter from his mom asking him for his picture. Since the only pictures he had were taken in the nude, he cut one in half and mailed her the photo from the waist up.

His mom called after receiving the photo and asked if his Grandma could have one too. The man didn't want to cut another photo in half, and since he knew Grandma couldn't see well, he sent the bottom half of the same photo.

A week later he got a letter from his grandmother: "Thank you so much for the lovely picture, but I think your haircut makes your nose look big."

A man was selling strawberries door-to-door. At one house a gorgeous woman answered the door. "I'd love to buy some strawberries!" she said. "Meet me around the back of the house at the back door."

The man went to the back of the house and found the woman standing in the doorway buck naked.

He immediately started crying.

"What's wrong?" the woman asked.

"Last week my house burned down," the man said. "Three days ago I was fired. Yesterday my wife left me, and I found out that she's been cheating on me for the past year. And now I'm going to get fucked out of my strawberries."

In the jungles of South America,
a group of scientists discovered an apelike creature that they were certain was the Missing
Link. But to prove their theory, a human had
to mate with the ape in order to see what
characteristics their offspring would have. So
the scientists put an ad in the paper that read,
"$5,000 to mate with ape."

The next morning a guy called up in
response to the ad and said he'd be willing to
be part of the experiment. "But," he said, "I have
three conditions."

"And what are they?" the scientists asked.

"First: My wife must never know. Second:
The children must be raised as Catholics. And
third: I need to pay you with my debit card."

A man is very horny, but also very broke. He manages to scrape up two dollars and goes to the local whorehouse. The madam looks at his money and laughs. She explains that the only service they offer for two dollars is the special cheapskate room. She ushers him into the room, and closes the door behind her. In the room, there's a full-length mirror and a duck.

The man has never considered fucking a duck before, and frankly it's a very homely mallard. But he's horny, and he'll try anything once. So he screws the duck.

A week later, the man is horny again, but even more broke. He goes to the whorehouse with his last dollar. The madam laughs and tells him that for one dollar he can't fuck anything, but he can see a good show.

She ushers him into a room where several men are gathered around a one-way window, masturbating furiously. On the other side of the window, the man sees a guy fucking a goat.

"Ugh, that's disgusting," he says, "how can you guys whack off to this?"

One of the spectators turns to him and says, "It's usually better. Last week they had a guy who was doing it with a duck!"

Every morning when Sam woke up, he began his day by ripping a gigantic fart in bed. It disgusted his wife, Martha. She warned him that one day he was going to fart his guts out, but her warnings had no effect on him.

One Thanksgiving morning Martha was up early preparing the turkey dinner when she thought of a devilish plan that just might stop Sam's disgusting habit. She took the giblets from the turkey, snuck into the bedroom, and cautiously slid them down the back of his shorts.

A few minutes later Sam woke up and cut a huge fart, as he did every morning. But this morning, he felt something strange when he rolled over onto his back. "Oh no," he muttered, and ran into the bathroom.

Even downstairs, Martha could hear his terrified scream.

She waited a few minutes, and then leisurely strolled upstairs to check on him. He was hunched on the toilet, pale and drenched in sweat. When he saw his wife he said, "My

God, Martha, you were right! I farted my guts out!" Holding up two fingers he continued, "But by the grace of God and these two fingers, I got them all back in!"

Two old priests were discussing the decline in morals in the world today. "I didn't sleep with my wife before I was married," the first clergyman said self-righteously. "Did you?"

"I don't know," said the other. "What was her maiden name?"

A guy and girl are making out in the back seat of a car, and things are starting to escalate.

"Put your finger inside me," the girl asks.

The guy eagerly slips his finger inside her, and she moans with pleasure.

"Put another finger inside me," she orders.

The guy slips in a second finger, and she moans louder.

"Put your whole hand inside me."

The guy puts his whole hand in.

"Put both hands inside me," the girl squeals.

The guy hesitates, but finally wedges both hands in.

"Now clap."

"I can't!" the guy protests.

"Tight, huh?" she smiles.

Pope Jokes

As head of the Roman Catholic Church and God's human representative here on the earth, the Pope serves many valuable functions: head of state, ecclesiastical jurist, and spiritual advisor for one of the world's largest religions. But none of these duties is as important as the Pope's primary role: an unlikely foil for ribald jokes. The Pope is a powerful dirty joke catalyst for a number of reasons:

1. He's pious
2. He wears a funny hat, and a silk robe like Grandma
3. He's often Polish
4. He loves to eat pussy

Put the Pope in almost any situation not involving holy rituals, and it's automatically amusing—can you imagine the Pope riding a skateboard?—but plunk him in the middle of a dirty joke, and major-league laughs are ensured. Blurt any one of these pope jokes during Mass, and you're sure to become Father Flannigan's new favorite drinking buddy.

The Pope was kidnapped by terrorists who wouldn't release him until he agreed to be photographed screwing a teenage girl. The terrorists figured that with such a photo in their possession, they could release the Pope but still have complete control over the Catholic Church.

The pontiff was outraged and refused. But after the terrorists made it clear that he would be killed unless he complied, he reluctantly agreed.

"However," said the Pope, "I will only cooperate on three conditions: One, the young girl must be blindfolded so she cannot see the horrible thing that's happening; two, the girl must be wearing earplugs so she can't hear what's happening."

"Fine, fine," the leader of the terrorists said. "What's the third condition?"

The Pope replied, "The girl's got to have real big tits."

The Pope is working on a crossword puzzle one Sunday afternoon when he reaches a real stumper. He thinks for a moment or two, scratches his head, and finally asks the cardinal, "Can you think of a four-letter word for 'woman' that ends in 'u-n-t'?"

"Aunt," replies the Cardinal.

"Ah, thanks," says the Pope. "Do you have an eraser?"

A cardinal is out fishing in a rowboat with a professional fisherman. The cardinal gets a bite on his line and hauls in a massive, beautiful fish.

"Wow!" exclaims the fisherman, "that's one big motherfucking fish!"

The cardinal is offended. "It's certainly big, but there's no need to swear."

The fisherman is mortified and tries to cover his gaffe. "You don't understand," he says. "That's the actual name of this species—like a catfish, or a carp, or a mackerel. It's a Motherfucking Fish."

"Oh, I see," says the cardinal. "Well, I guess you're right then, it is one big Motherfucker."

The cardinal takes the fish back to his church. The Pope is going to dine at their church that night, and since the cardinal wants to do something special, he tells one of the bishops to clean the fish so they can serve it for dinner. "Here," says the cardinal, "would you mind cleaning this Motherfucker?"

"Uh, certainly, Father," the bishop stammers, "but you might want to watch your language."

"It's quite all right," says the cardinal. "It's a Motherfucking Fish, that's its name."

The bishop cleans the fish and then gives it to one of the sisters to cook. "Excuse me sister, would you mind cooking this Motherfucking Fish for the Pope's dinner?"

The sister blushes. "It's a lovely fish, but you should mind your language, Padre."

"Oh, no, you don't understand," says the bishop. "The scientific name for this creature is the Motherfucking Fish."

That evening, the Pope arrived with a huge procession. Every candle in the church was lit, and the dining room was set with golden plates and pewter wine decanters. The meal had a dozen delicious courses, each more succulent than the previous, and the cardinal told the sister to bring out the fish last. At the end of the meal, the sister finally brought out the massive fish on a platter.

"My, what a beautiful fish!" the Pope said.

The cardinal leaned in and said, "Can you believe that I caught that Motherfucking Fish myself, Your Holiness?"

The priest also wanted to impress the Pope, so he said, "I cleaned the Motherfucker."

As the sister put the platter down, she demurely admitted, "And I cooked this Motherfucker, so I hope you enjoy it, Your Holiness."

The Pope was stunned into silence. He looked around the room to see if anybody else had heard what they said. Then he leaned in and whispered, "Bring some more wine. You fuckers are my kind of people."

A woman told her lawyer she was divorcing her husband on the grounds of hobosexuality.

Her lawyer said, "I think you mean 'homosexuality.'"

"No," the woman said, "he likes to fuck hobos."*

---

*Even though this joke doesn't feature the Pope, it is included in this section because it was actually written by Pope Pius XII, intended as a parable demonstrating the evils of both homosexuality and divorce. As a result of this joke, Pius XII became the patron saint of hobos, who still carve his crude likeness on the sides of boxcars to this day.

A couple took their young son

for his first visit to the circus, and their seats happened to be next to the elephant pen. When his father got up to buy some popcorn, the boy asked his mother, "Mom, what's that long thing hanging off the elephant?"

"That's the elephant's trunk, dear," she replied.

"No, not that," the boy said.

"Oh, that's the elephant's tail."

"No, Mom. Down underneath."

His mother blushed and said, "Oh, that's nothing."

A moment later the father returned, and the mother left to get a soda. The boy repeated his questions to the father.

"That's the elephant's trunk," said the father.

"Dad, I know what an elephant's trunk is. What's the thing at the other end?"

"That's the elephant's tail."

"No, down underneath."

The father finally realized what the boy was talking about, and said "Oh, that's the elephant's penis."

"Dad," the boy asked, "how come when I asked Mom, she said it was nothing?"

The man shrugged and replied, "Son, I've spoiled that woman."

A young man decided that he wasn't adequately endowed, so he went to a doctor and asked to have his penis surgically enlarged.

The doctor told the young man that the best way to lengthen his penis was a radically advanced type of surgery that involved implanting a section of a baby elephant's trunk into his cock.

The patient thought the surgery was an extreme solution, but the doctor assured him that it was completely safe and the best way to lengthen his member.

Sure enough, the operation was performed without any complications, and after a few weeks of recuperation the young man decided it was time to try out his new accoutrement.

He took a beautiful young woman he knew out to dinner at an elegant restaurant. The date was going smoothly. They were having a lovely conversation when his new organ, which had been comfortably resting in his left pants leg, snaked out over the edge of the table, grabbed a hard roll, and quickly disappeared back under the table.

"Wow!" said the girl, truly impressed. "Can you do that again?"

"I could," he said, "but I don't know if my asshole can stand another hard roll."

A doctor, a lawyer, and an architect were arguing about who had the smartest dog. They decided to settle the argument by seeing whose dog could perform the most impressive trick.

"Do your trick, Rover," said the architect.

Rover trotted over to a table and, in only a few minutes, constructed a quarter-scale model of St. Peter's Basilica out of balsa wood. Everyone agreed it was an exact rendition, and the architect gave Rover a cookie.

"Do your trick, Fido," said the doctor.

An anaesthetized patient was wheeled in. Fido performed a triple-bypass surgery. Everyone conceded it was an impressive surgery, and the doctor gave Fido a cookie.

"Okay Toby, do your trick," ordered the lawyer.

Toby fucked the two other dogs, took their cookies, and went out to lunch.

One winter morning, the President of the United States woke up and saw that someone had written in pee in the snow outside the White House window, "The President sucks." Furious, he summoned the Secret Service, the police, and the FBI and told them they had better discover the culprit—fast.

That afternoon an embarrassed officer arrived in the Oval Office to give the president the results of their investigation. "We have definitively established that it's the vice president's urine," he said.

"Ah-ha!" said the president.

"But," the officer continued, "I'm afraid it's the First Lady's handwriting."

An elephant was walking through the jungle when he got a nasty thorn stuck in his foot. He was unable to extract it and had given up all hope when an ant came along the same path. "I don't suppose you could get this thorn out of my foot, could you?" asked the elephant.

"I'll pull the thorn out of your foot if you let me fuck you in the ass," said the ant.

The elephant's foot hurt badly, and he figured he wouldn't even notice getting fucked by an ant, so he told the ant he had a deal.

After a few minutes the ant worked the thorn free. "Are you ready to get nailed, elephant?" he squealed triumphantly.

The elephant was honest, so he kept his side of the bargain. He stood very still while the ant made his laborious way around to his ass, heaved his tail out of the way, and began fucking him in the ass.

A monkey high in a tree witnessed the entire transaction. Unable to contain his hysteria at the sight of the ant pounding away at the elephant's rear, he began tossing coconuts down at the beast. One coconut hit the elephant square on the head, and he howled in pain.

"Take it all, bitch!" squealed the ant.

A young man went to his doctor

for a routine checkup, and when he came in for the results, the doctor said gravely, "Jerry, I think you'd better sit down. I've got some good news and some bad news."

"All right doc," said Jerry. "Give me the bad news first."

"You've got cancer," said the doctor. "Brain cancer. It's spreading at an unbelievably rapid rate, it's totally inoperable, and you've got about two weeks to live."

"Jesus," said Jerry. "What's the good news?"

"Did you see the receptionist in the front office?"

"Yeah," said Jerry.

"The one with the big tits?"

"Yeah."

"And the long blonde hair?"

"Yeah, yeah," Jerry said impatiently.

The doctor leaned forward with a smile. "I'm fucking her!"

A married woman is having an affair. Whenever her lover comes over, she puts her nine-year-old son in the closet. One day, the woman hears her husband's car in the driveway, and she quickly hides her lover in the closet, too.

Inside the closet, the little boy says, "It's dark in here, isn't it?"

"Yes, it is," the man replies.

"You wanna buy a baseball?" the little boy asks.

"No, thanks," the man replies.

"I think you want to buy a baseball," the little extortionist continues.

The man considers his delicate position and relents. "Okay, how much?"

"A hundred dollars," the little boy replies.

"A hundred dollars!" the man repeats incredulously. But the boy is impassive, and the man complies to protect his hiding place.

The following week, the lover is visiting the woman again when her husband arrives home unexpectedly. Again, she puts her lover in the closet with her little boy.

"It's dark in here, isn't it?" the boy starts off.

"Yes, it is," replies the man.

"Wanna buy a baseball glove?" the little boy asks.

"Okay, how much?" he responds wearily.

"Two hundred dollars," the boy replies.

The lover can hear the husband through the closet door, so he ponies up and gives the kid the dough.

The next weekend, the little boy's father says, "Hey son. Go get your ball and glove and we'll play some catch."

"I can't, I sold them for three hundred bucks," replies the little boy.

"Three hundred dollars! That's thievery!" the father says. "I'm taking you to the church right now so you can confess your sin and ask forgiveness."

The father marches his son to church.

The little boy sits down in the confessional, draws the curtain, and says, "It's dark in here, isn't it?"

The priest says, "Don't start that shit in here now."

A woman goes to her doctor to get some relief for the bruises on her knees.

"How did you get these bruises?" asks the doctor.

Embarrassed, the woman says, "Well, you see, Doctor, when I, uh, make love with my, uh, well . . ."

"Oh, I understand," says the doctor. "Just change positions until those bruises heal."

"Oh no, doctor, I can't do that. My dog's breath is atrocious!"

Kids Say the Darndest Motherfucking Things

There is a large and frightening group of dirty jokes that involve young children behaving like foul-mouthed, world-weary sailors. These jokes are similar to dirty Pope jokes in that their humor is derived from the unexpected behavior of the main character: A mother finishes breastfeeding her baby, and instead of burping or cooing contentedly, the baby asks (in a Brooklyn accent), "What do I have to do to get past second base with you?"

Sweet, doe-eyed children commit all sorts of deplorable acts in these jokes: They swear, drink whiskey, buy hookers, and generally behave like a fifth Baldwin brother.

There is a significant difference between these jokes and the Pope jokes, though. Whereas it's unlikely that the Pope would buy a hooker, it is virtually impossible for a toddler to do so. Where would he get the money? How would he get to the whore-house? Where are his parents?

These are troubling questions that you should not ask. The famous comedy scholar Bing Supernova spent his last twenty years in jail after conducting an experiment to see if the infamous "Womb with a View" joke was physically possible.

Although real kids certainly aren't as decadent and depraved as the ones depicted in these jokes, they're also not as innocent as you might think. Babies spend all day sucking titties and napping. In fact, depending on who you are, a five-year-old child's last experience with a vagina may have been more recent than your own—although they were crawling out, while you spend every waking moment trying desperately to get back in.

Oh, the irony!

A woman and her eight-year-old daughter were walking along a country road when they saw a stallion mounting a mare. "Mommy," the little girl asked, "what are those horses doing?"

The mother stuttered a moment before she came up with a creative answer. "The horse on top hurt his hoof, and the one underneath is helping him back to the barn."

The little girl shook her head and said, "That's the same way it is with people. You try to help somebody and you end up getting fucked."

A little boy walks into an ice-cream store wearing a cowboy hat and a pair of six-shooters. The woman behind the counter can't help smiling at the tough expression on his chubby little face.

"Hello there, cowboy," she says. "What can I get for you?"

The kid bellies up to the counter. "I'll have an ice-cream sundae with butterscotch, cherries, nuts, sprinkles, and chocolate syrup."

"Do you want your nuts crushed?" the clerk asks.

The little boy whips out his guns, points them at her, and says, "Do you want your tits shot off?"

Eight-year-old Paul and six-year-old Bryn were hiding in their big sister's closet as she entertained her boyfriend. They heard a lot of panting and moaning, and then their sister sighed, "Oh Joey, you're in where no man's been before."

Paul turned to Bryn and said, "Wow, he must be fucking her in the ass!"

One day Father McGonigal was walking through the park when he saw a picturesque tableau: A beautiful little girl in a white lace dress, playing under a tree with an adorable puppy.

Father McGonigal walked over and asked the girl what her name was.

"Blossom," she replied.

"What a pretty name for a pretty girl," said Father McGonigal. "How did your parents choose such a sweet name?"

"Well, one day when I was still in my mommy's tummy, she was lying under this tree right here, and a blossom fell and landed on her stomach. She thought it was a message from God and decided that if I was a girl, my name would be Blossom."

The priest was genuinely touched by the child's story. Blossom's puppy hopped and rolled in the tall grass. "What's the name of your little dog?" he asked.

"Porky," the girl replied.

"And why did you name him that?" the priest asked.

"Because he likes to fuck pigs."

A little boy walks in on his mother and father having sex. His mother is on top of his father, bobbing up and down.

The little boy asks, "What are you doing, Mommy?"

The mother thinks quickly and replies, "Daddy is getting fat, so I thought I would try to flatten his tummy."

The little boy says, "I don't know why you bother. The minute you leave for work, the maid comes in and blows it right back up again."

A man works for many years in a pickle factory. He works the machine right next to the pickle slicer. At night he has sex dreams about the pickle slicer, and he wakes up feeling guilty but thrilled. One day he finally goes nuts, and he starts to kiss the pickle slicer when he thinks no one is looking. Lust overpowers his reason, and he puts his dick in the pickle slicer. At that moment the boss happens to be passing by and sees the man attacking the pickle slicer. The boss calls the man a pervert and fires him.

When the man goes home, his wife asks him why he's home so early. "I went crazy and tried to make love to the pickle slicer," he replies. "The boss caught me and fired me."

"Oh my god!" screams the wife. She pulls down her husband's pants to inspect the damage, but he appears to be fine. "Well, thank the Lord you weren't hurt," she says. "But what happened to the pickle slicer?"

The man smiles sheepishly and says, "The boss fired her, too."

A blind man walks into a diner

and takes a seat at the counter. The owner asks if he'd like to have the menu read to him.

"That's not necessary," the blind man says, "just give me a dirty fork from one of the tables."

The owner grabs a dirty fork off a plate and hands it to the blind man, who puts it under his nose and inhales deeply.

"Hmm, meatloaf with garlic mashed potatoes. That smells good. I'll take a plate of that."

The diner owner is amazed at the blind man's sense of smell, and he orders him the food.

A few days later, the blind man comes in again and once again asks for a dirty fork, which the owner promptly plucks from a plate.

"Mm, grilled cheese with French fries," says the blind man, "I'll take that."

The owner is so astounded by the blind man's sense of smell, he starts to wonder if perhaps he's actually faking his disability.

A couple days later the blind man comes in again. As usual he asks for a fork to smell, but this time the diner owner has devised a test to see if the man's sense of smell is as keen as he claims. He goes into the back and says to his wife, "Here, rub this fork on your pussy."

He takes the fork to the blind man, who inhales deeply. The blind man breaks into a smile and says, "I didn't know Karen worked here!"

Mickey Mouse stood in divorce court, waiting for the judge's verdict.

"Mickey Mouse," commanded the judge, "I cannot grant you a divorce, since the court has found Minnie Mouse to be mentally competent."

"But, Your Honor, I didn't say Minnie was crazy. I said she was fucking Goofy!"

A lion is fucking a zebra. Suddenly he sees his wife approaching over the hill, about to catch him red-handed.

"Quick," he says to the zebra. "Pretend I'm killing you."

A young man who is very bad with money goes off to college in another state. After only one month he has spent all his money, and he has to ask his father for more. His father agrees to send some money but warns him that this will be the last loan until next semester.

Unfortunately, the boy has spent everything a month later, so he tries to devise a scheme to get more money from his dad. Remembering that his father would do anything for the family dog, the boy calls his father and says, "Dad, there's a professor here who will teach Toby to speak for a thousand bucks." After a little persuasion, the father agrees to send Toby to college for speech lessons.

After a couple of months, the young man burns through the thousand dollars, so he calls his father again. This time he says, "Dad, Toby did so well with the speech lessons that the professor feels he has the potential to learn how to read as well. It will only cost another thousand bucks." Again he persuades his father, and the money arrives.

Freshman year finally ends, and the father is excited to have his son bring their dog home for the summer so he can hear him talk and watch him read. Desperate to hide his deception, the boy gives away Toby to a nice family and then makes a phone call to his dad.

"Dad, I've got some bad news for you, but it's a long story, so maybe you should sit down."

Silence on the other end of the phone.

The son continues. "I was in the bathroom shaving, and Toby was in the bathtub reading the *New York Times*. Suddenly he says 'Gee, do you think your mother will ever find out about all the times Dad fucked around with his secretary?' I was so surprised that my hand slipped, and I dropped the electric razor in the bathtub. Toby was electrocuted, and he's dead."

His father finally breaks the silence on the other end of the phone and says, "And you're sure he's really dead?"

This guy is grocery shopping

when an extremely attractive woman walks up
to him.

"Excuse me," she says, "I know this is
rather forward, but . . . I think you're the
father of one of my children."

The guy goes pale as a sheet. "Oh, geez.
Are you sure?"

"Yes, I'm positive I remember you," she said.

The woman is extremely attractive, with
large breasts, penetrating eyes, and pouting,
tender lips. The guy tries to remember where
he knows her from, and then it hits him. "Oh
my god," he says. "You aren't . . . the dancer
from John's bachelor party three years ago?
The one who rubbed peanut butter on my
balls and had a dog lick it off on stage? I
remember we went back to your apartment,
where you blindfolded me and made me fish a
soggy banana out of the toilet bowl with my
teeth, and then we fucked while your room-
mate drilled me in the pooper with a strap-on.

I'm not surprised you got pregnant; I came so hard I remember a little even squirted out your nose." He laughs.

"Actually," the woman said, "I meant that your son Jeremy is in my English class."

An Australian missionary was dragged out of his bed by an angry mob of Aborigines one night. Before he knew what was happening, he was beaten and tied to a post. The chief of the tribe drew a knife and advanced toward him. "What's going on here?" the missionary cried.

The Aborigine chief said, "One of our women just gave birth to a white baby. Since you're the only white man in many days' walk, it must be yours."

The missionary called the chief close and said, "Wait a minute, you don't understand. Let me explain something to you. You know that flock of pure white sheep I keep? Well one of them gave birth to a black lamb, even though there aren't any black sheep around."

The chief thought about that for a moment, and then demanded that the missionary be cut free. As the missionary was rubbing his wrists, the chief whispered to him, "I keep your secret, you keep mine."

Three women are in the locker room getting ready to play racquetball when a masked man runs in, stark naked, dick flopping around.

The first woman looks at his dick and says, "Well, it's certainly not my husband."

The second woman says, "No, it isn't."

The third woman says, "That guy's not even a member of this club."

A man called his doctor and told him he had a problem with his wife. "Every morning," the man said, "She has a bowel movement at seven o'clock on the dot."

"It's not unusual to have a regular schedule for your bowel movements," the doctor said. "In fact, it's healthy."

"But Doc, we don't get out of bed until nine."

Two guys were walking down the street when they saw a dog licking his dick. "Boy," one guy marveled, "I wish I could do that."

"I bet you could," his friend replied. "But you'd probably have to pet him a little first."

A man is shaving with a straight-edge razor when it slips out of his hands and chops off his penis. Losing blood and slipping into shock, he barely has the presence of mind to pick up his penis, stuff it in his pocket, and run outside to hail a cab.

The cab drops him off at the emergency room. He rushes in, tells the surgeon what has happened, and desperately asks if they'll be able to reattach his cock.

"Yes," the surgeon says, "if we work quickly. Give it to me."

The man reaches into his pocket and deposits its contents into the surgeon's hand.

"This isn't a penis," says the surgeon. "It's a cigar!"

The man smacks his forehead. "Oh my God," he moans, "I must have smoked it in the cab."

Steve's elbow hurt. He complained to his friend, who recommended he visit a swami who lived in a nearby cave.

"All you have to do is leave a sample of urine outside his cave. You won't see the swami, but he will meditate on the sample, diagnose your problem, and prescribe a cure. It's fucking incredible: He's never wrong, and it costs only ten dollars."

Steve figured he'd give it a shot, so he filled a jar with urine and left it outside the swami's cave on top of a ten-dollar bill. When he returned to the cave the next day, there was a note that said, "You have tennis elbow. Soak your arm in warm water. Don't do any strenuous exercise. It will heal in a week."

Later that evening, Steve started to suspect that the whole swami thing just might be a prank his friend was pulling. He could have easily written the note and left it outside the cave himself. What a jerk! Well, two could play this game.

The next day Steve left another jar of liquid outside the cave. This one contained a concoction of several different fluids: tap water, a urine sample from his dog, and urine samples from his wife and son. To top it off, he jerked off in it, shook the whole thing up, and left it outside the cave with ten dollars. Then he called his friend and told him that he was having some more health problems and that he had left another sample for the swami.

The next day Steve returned to the cave and found a note that said, "Your tap water has high levels of lead. Get a water purifier. Your dog has worms. Get him vitamins. Your son is hooked on meth. Get him into rehab. Your wife is pregnant with twins. They aren't yours. Get a lawyer. And if you don't stop jerking off, your tennis elbow will never get better."

A young nun was assigned by the Mother Superior to help old Father O'Mally with his Sunday night bath. The next morning, the older nun asked the young girl if she had had any difficulties.

"Oh no," the nun smiled. "As a matter of fact, I attained eternal salvation."

The Mother was puzzled. "What do you mean?"

"Well, Father O'Mally took my hand and put it between his legs. Then a miracle happened: The key to heaven grew in my hand. Father O'Mally said that if the key to heaven fit in my lock, I'd be saved forever. And it fit! Although it was a little snug."

"That lying snake!" The Mother Superior spat bitterly. "For fifteen years he's been telling me that was Gabriel's Horn between his legs, and I've been blowing it as hard as I could."

Fred, Charlie, and Jason were playing golf together like they did every Sunday. On the fourth hole, Fred chipped a shot into the rough. "You guys play on," he insisted. "I'll catch up with you."

Half an hour later Fred still hadn't caught up to them, so Charlie said, "I'll go back and check on him."

Jason played on for a while, but after another twenty minutes neither Fred nor Charlie had caught up to him. Finally, he turned around to see what was holding them up.

An astonishing sight greeted him when he returned to the fourth hole: Poor Fred was bent over the back seat of his golf cart, and Charlie was fucking him in the ass.

"Charlie, what the hell are you doing?" Jason yelled, breaking into a run.

"It was horrible," gasped a red-face Charlie, still thrusting. "When I got here, Fred had a massive heart attack."

"You're supposed to give him heart massage, you idiot," cried Jason, "and mouth-to-mouth resuscitation."

"I know that," Charlie said indignantly. "How do you think this got started?"

One morning a young woman

walked out her front door and noticed a strange little man perched on a rock in her garden. He was smoking a long pipe, wore a pointed hat, and had shrewd, wizened features.

Quietly, she snuck up behind the little man and said, "Gotcha! You're a goblin and I caught you!"

The goblin was pissed. "All right, yes, fine. You got me. So what?"

"You can't fool me," said the woman. "I know the rules. If someone catches you, you have to grant them three wishes."

"That's true," said the goblin. "What are your three wishes?"

The woman thought for a minute and then said, "I want a million dollars, a 100-acre horse ranch, and a diamond the size of a baseball."

"You got it," said the goblin, who clapped his hands and did a little jig. "But first, you have to have sex with me all night. That's the only way to make the wishes come true."

The woman wasn't too keen on the idea, but she agreed.

The next morning the goblin woke up the woman. "Tell me," he asks, "how old are you?"

"I'm 25 years old," she said.

"Fuck me," said the little man. "Twenty-five and you still believe in goblins."

A young man and his fiancée are visiting her family's farm. The young man knows nothing about farming, and he gets the feeling that her family doesn't approve of their daughter marrying a city slicker. So that night he decides to impress the family by waking up before everyone else the next morning, milking a cow, and bringing in the fresh milk for breakfast.

He wakes up at the crack of dawn and sneaks out to the barn. He's never milked a cow before, and it's much more difficult than he expected. But eventually he gets the hang of it, and after a lot of hard work he fills a whole bucket. He carries the bucket back to the house and into the kitchen, where everybody is already sitting around the table eating pancakes.

"Where were you?" his fiancée asks.

He wipes the sweat off his forehead melodramatically and plops the bucket on the counter. "Well, you might think I'm just a city slicker, but I thought it might be nice to have some fresh milk with our breakfast, so I went out and milked the cow." He dips a glass into the bucket and takes a hearty gulp.

"Cow?" the father looks up from the table. "We don't own a cow. All we have is a bull."

After months of working in the most desolate region of the desert, three American men were desperate for female company. However, they were forbidden to talk to the local women. Despite warnings that there would be grave consequences if they disobeyed the law, they tried to pick up some Arab women and were promptly arrested by the police and hauled in front of the local sheik.

"Infidel dogs," the sheik swore. "You were warned not to touch our women! Now you will pay the price: You will spend the rest of your lives squatting to piss like a woman."

The three men begged for mercy as the guards tied them to columns in the palace's courtyard. The sheik walked up to the first man and asked, "What is the profession of your father, swine?"

"He's a lumberjack," the man said.

The sheik slapped him across the face. "You have disgraced him," the sheik said. "So your penis will be chopped off with an ax."

The man was dragged off by the guards, kicking and screaming.

The sheik went to the second man and asked the same question. The man didn't want to talk, but after some persuasion he replied, "My father was a fireman."

"In that case, we will burn off your prick." The sheik said, as the man was untied and dragged away.

The sheik turned to the third man and was surprised to see that he was laughing. "What's so funny?" the sheik demanded.

"My father made lollipops!" the man cried.

This woman is morbidly obese.

She is so fat that one day her ass gets stuck in the toilet. She struggles and struggles but can't extricate herself. She yells to her husband, "Herman! Help me! Help!"

Herman runs in and sees her predicament. He tries to get her unstuck—he pulls her arms, he pulls her legs, but she doesn't budge. He greases her great flanks with butter and even uses a crowbar, but her ass remains firmly lodged in the bowl. Finally, he gives up. "We're just going to have to call a plumber and have him dismantle the bowl," he says.

"You can't! My mother gave us this toilet as a wedding present!" his wife wails. But Herman is already in the other room placing the call.

A few minutes later the plumber pulls into the driveway. The woman suddenly realizes that she has no pants on. "The plumber can't see me like this! Give me something to cover up with!"

Herman thinks fast, takes off his yarmulke, and puts it over his wife's vagina. The plumber opens the bathroom door and surveys the scene. After a long pause, he turns to the husband and says, "Well, I think I can get your wife out. But I'm pretty sure the rabbi's a goner."

This guy walks into a bar. There's only one other patron in the bar, and he looks lonely, so the first guy tries to strike up a conversation.

"Hi, my name's Mike. What's your name?"

The guy turns and says, "Tom." Then he points out the window and says, "You see that wall out there? I built that wall with my own bare hands."

Mike looks out the window and says "Well, it's a very nice wall."

"You're damn right it is! Tallest brick wall in three counties!" Tom screams. "But do people call me 'Tom the Mason'? No, they don't." He points out the window again and says, "You see that sign across the street? Well I painted that sign. And it's the most beautifully painted sign in the whole town! But do they call me 'Tom the Sign painter'? No, they don't."

"Well, that's just—"

"And do you see this bar we're drinking at?" Tom interrupted. "I carved this very bar with my own hands! All the inlaid wood and the brass accents. But do they call me 'Tom the Carpenter'? No, they don't."

He drained his glass and shook his head. "But you fuck one little sheep . . ."

A young man wanted to ensure that his virgin bride's sexual inexperience wouldn't be a cause of any tension or trouble. He explained that he didn't want her to ever feel pressured into having sex with him—he wanted it to come of her own free will.

"That's so sweet of you," the bride said. "I really appreciate that."

He kissed her on the nose. "As a matter of fact, darling, I've devised a code so that when we're in bed at night, you can tell me whether or not you want to have sex. Here's how it works: When you want to have sex, pull my penis once; when you don't want to have sex, pull my penis one hundred times."

Dr. Gerben is an internationally renowned expert in a highly specialized field of cardiology. He received his PhD and MD in his hometown and went on to practice in New York City. He wrote a revolutionary medical paper and was asked to read it at an international medical conference that was coincidentally held in his hometown.

The conference is very prestigious, and it is held in the town's opera house. The men are all wearing tuxedos, the women are wearing gowns. As the doctor sits in the audience waiting to give his speech, he grows very nervous. His stomach is upset, and he suddenly feels an overwhelming urge to shit. Just as he's about to get up to use the bathroom, he's called to the stage to give his speech.

When Dr. Gerben takes the stage and places his papers on the lectern in the front of the microphone, he drops his pen. He bends over to pick it up, unwittingly placing his ass very close to the microphone. At that very

moment, he lets loose an ungodly fart. A fart
that roars up from the literal bowels of hell and
gallops through the room, shaking chandeliers,
rattling windows—echoing through the entire
hall, amplified by the microphone. Furthermore,
it's clear from the wetness of the sound and the
spreading brown stain on the back his pants
that he's shit himself.

The doctor is so ashamed that he runs off
the stage, darts out a back door, and swears
never to return to his hometown again.

Many, many years go by, and his mother
falls ill. He has no choice but to return home
to care for her. He checks into a local hotel
under the name Haines and arrives under cover
of darkness. A bright and friendly young clerk
greets him at the reception desk and says,
"Good evening Dr. Haines. Have you ever
been to our lovely town before?"

"Yes, as a matter of fact, I grew up here,"
Dr. Gerben says. "But I haven't visited in a
long time."

"Why not?" the clerk asks.

"Well, a number of years ago an embarrassing thing happened here, and I didn't feel I could come back and face the people in the town."

The clerk says, "I know you're a distinguished doctor and I'm just a kid, but let me give you some advice: A lot of times when I do something that I think is really embarrassing, it turns out that nobody else even noticed. I bet that's the case for whatever you think is so embarrassing."

"No, I doubt anyone has forgotten this," the doctor said.

The young man asked, "Was it a long time ago?"

"Yes, it was a long time ago," the doctor replied.

"Was it before or after the Gerben Fart?"

What's the difference between jelly and jam?

You can't jelly your dick in someone's ass.

Extremely Dirty Jokes: A Warning

Brave reader, you and I stand at the edge of a perilous precipice. The next—and final—section of this book holds the dirtiest, foulest, most reprehensible jokes we could legally publish in this country (God Bless America). We had to sequester them in the back of book, otherwise they would beat the shit out of all the other jokes. "Oh, a guy gets a boner in your punchline? That's quaint. My punchline can cause birth defects in unborn infants."

I know that sounds enticing, and your curiosity is piqued, but I warn you—like a scabby old crone in a black cloak, I shake my bony fingers at you and shriek "Abandon all hope, ye who pass this page!" This section is like the mythical vessel of Pandora's box. Once you turn this page, you cannot turn it back. Once read, these jokes cannot be unread. Seared onto your brain like acid etched into a photographic plate, they will linger in the dark corners of your mind, popping up when you least expect them—at your child's christening, during your wedding vows, or every single time you hug your mother from now on.

Many of these jokes are rarely even printed on paper. They're passed from death row inmate to death row inmate via Morse code, tapped on stone over the course of a black and sleepless night.

That said, I suppose there's the possibility that, for some of you, these ultra-dirty jokes may not live up to the hype. You Atrocity-of-the-Month club members may read the soul melting filth on the following pages and scoff, "These jokes read like my diary! Murder/incest/shit/fuck is my shopping list." For those of you who require even sterner stuff than what follows on these pages, I can only say: Damn, girl.

A guy is locked up in the state penitentiary doing five to ten for armed robbery. He misses a lot of things during those years: fresh air, home-cooked food, a warm bed. But the entire time, dominating his waking thoughts, the thing he misses most is eating pussy.

When the day of his release finally arrives, he walks out of the prison with the new suit and ten dollars the officials gave him, and he goes straight to the nearest whorehouse. He slams down his ten-dollar bill on the front desk and says, "I wanna eat some pussy!"

"Where've you been?" says the greasy fellow behind the desk. "Ten dollars these days don't buy more than a close look."

"Listen, buddy," says the ex-con, pulling him out of his chair by his nose, "I wanna eat some pussy, and I want it now."

"Okay, okay," gasps the proprietor, "I'll see what I can do." He leads the ex-con through some stained, tattered red curtains to the very back of the whore-house, into a grimy room where a bedraggled whore lays spread-eagled on a filthy bed. "She's yours for the ten dollars," says the proprietor.

The ex-con dives in and starts eating pussy like an animal. After a while, though, he comes across a piece of egg. "That's funny," he thinks to himself, "I don't think I had eggs for breakfast." But he spits it out and keeps eating away.

A minute later he finds a piece of chipped beef wedged between his front teeth. "I'm sure I haven't eaten chipped beef this week," he thinks, but dives back in.

Then he finds some corn.

"I know I haven't eaten any corn lately," he says, sitting up. "I think I'm going to be sick."

"Ya know," says the whore, "that's what the last guy said."

A guy picked up an older woman in a bar and took her back to his place for an evening of fucking. As the groaning and grinding increased in intensity, his lips strayed to the crone's sagging tit. Wrapping his lips around the nipple, he began to suck vigorously—and got a mouthful of liquid.

"Jesus," he exclaimed, "Aren't you too old to be giving milk?"

"Yes, baby," she replied, "but I'm not too old to have cancer."

At the crack of dawn one morning, a husband wakes up his wife and says, "Honey, we're going fishing today—you, me, and the dog."

The wife tells the husband that she does not like fishing. "You know I hate the outdoors. Why don't you and Toby go without me?"

"Look! We're going fishing, and that's final."

The wife protests and says fishing is the last thing she wants to do; she'll do anything other than that.

"All right then," the husband says, "I'll give you three choices: One, you come fishing with me and the dog; two, you give me a blow job; or three, you take it up the ass."

The wife says, "But I don't want to do any of those things!"

"Well you're going to have to pick one," the husband says. "Marriage is a compromise. I'm going to the garage to sort my fishing tackle, and when I come back I expect you to have made up your mind."

The wife meditates on what a sham her marriage has become, but when her husband returns she relents and says, "All right, I'll give you a blow job."

"Great," the husband says, and drops his pants.

The wife starts sucking his dick, but immediately stops and says, "Yuck! It tastes like shit!"

"Yeah," he says. "The dog didn't want to go fishing either."

A ninety-five-year-old mother lived with her sixty-year-old son. One Mother's Day her son offered to fuck her as a present. She was grateful, but a few minutes after his wrinkled Charleston Chew entered her withered, raw turkey vagina, she shit all over herself.

The son rolled off and said, "Mom, why the hell did you do that?"

The old lady said, "Son, I'm too old to come, but you know I love you so much that I had to do something."

Write Your Own Dirty Joke!

Here we are, dear reader, at the end of the book. "What," you say. "So soon?" I know, time flies when you're laughing at unspeakable sex acts.

Luckily for you, there is one way to make this book last forever: Have your memory erased, then read the book again. Wait, now that I think of it, there's another way, but it's a little bit harder: Write your *own* dirty jokes.

I know what you're thinking: "Doogie, if I could write my own dirty jokes, I wouldn't have bought this book full of witty wise-cracks that I can memorize and pass off as my own brilliant chestnuts. . . . Wait a minute, can you hear my thoughts? Get out of my head! Aaaah!"

Fortunately, I've created an idiot-proof (that's you), step-by-step, insta-joke™ system for unimaginative hacks such as yourself. To "create" "your" own "unique" dirty joke, simply mix and match from the options below.

This guy walks into a (*bar / doctor's office / confessional box / his own bedroom*), and is (*startled / pleased / apoplectic / aroused*) to find a (*alligator / eight-inch-tall man wearing a tuxedo / legless hooker / Shetland pony*) there. Somewhere in the distance, a dog barks. A snatch of some memory from his childhood floats into his mind, then disappears on the (*breeze / wind / wings of a dove / queef of an angel*). He walks up to the (*bartender / receptionist / priest / horse's asshole*) and says (*"I'm glad I wore my loafers," / "I'd like a womb with a view," / "I'll have a shot of bull sperm," / "Jane, stop this crazy thing!"*).

Just then, a (*blind man / incredibly attractive nurse / genie / Polish lumberjack*) appears, vigorously (*waving / chewing / sniffing / scrapbooking*) a shoebox full of pussy lips.

"Ah Christ," the guy says, "not again!" (*Make sure you say this last line with a heavy Jewish accent.*)

Congratulations! Go pass off this dirty joke as your own, and none of your (*frat brothers* / *Facebook friends* / *parishioners* / *coworkers*) will call you a (*queer* / *humorless crone* / *Baptist* / *joy-sucking black hole*) ever again.

About the Editor

Doogie Horner is a stand-up comedian and writer based in Philadelphia. His books include *The First-Timer's Kit* (Quirk, 2008) and *Everything Explained Through Flowcharts* (HarperCollins, 2010). His writing has also appeared in *McSweeney's Joke Book of Book Jokes* (Vintage, 2008), and numerous other publications.

Acknowledgments

Special thanks to all the friends who shared their dirty jokes with me, especially Dave Walk, Chip Chantry, Roger Weaver, Conrad Roth, and everyone at the Ministry of Secret Jokes.